Field Marshal Plaek Phibun Songkhram

LEADERS OF ASIA
General Editor: K.G. Tregonning

Field Marshal Plaek Phibun Songkhram: B.J. Terwiel
Jinnah: K. McPherson
Sun Yat-sen: Richard Rigby
Jawaharlal Nehru of India 1889—1964: Ian Copland

Forthcoming titles in the series

Prasad: Gil McDonald
Tilak: Richard Cashman
Gandhi: Hugh Owen

Field Marshal
Plaek Phibun Songkhram

B.J. Terwiel

Leaders of Asia Series

University of Queensland Press

Typeset by Bacchus Type & Offset Pty Ltd, Brisbane
Printed and bound by Southwood Press Pty Ltd, Sydney

Distributed in the United Kingdom, Europe, the Middle East,
Africa, and the Caribbean by Prentice-Hall International,
International Book Distributors Ltd, 66 Wood Lane End, Hemel
Hempstead, Herts., England

National Library of Australia
Cataloguing-in-Publication data

Terwiel, Barend Jan, 1941-
     Field Marshal Plaek Phibun Songkhram, Thailand's Prime
     Minister from 1938-44 and from 1948-57.

     (Leaders of Asia; no. 2 ISSN 0157-3268)
     Bibliography
     ISBN 0 7022 1509 0

     1. Phibun Songkhram, Luang, 1897-1964. 2. Prime
     Ministers - Thailand - Biography. 3. Thailand -
     Politics and government. I. Title. (Series)

959.304'0924

Introduction

This book is one of a series of monographs entitled Leaders of Asia. Each book is a brief but stimulating study of a man or woman who has contributed to the shape of Asia. Through a study of his career will emerge a greater knowledge of his country's place in the contemporary scene.

It is vital for Australians to understand the region of their future. It has been neglected in our studies for too long. This book, as part of a series, is aimed at enriching our awareness of the multi-cultural, turbulent, dynamic nations of Asia which are now impinging ever more steadily on our national consciousness.

As a biography this book can be read by itself with enjoyment. History is not merely the story of great men, but there is hardly a better way of studying it than by reading of them. If you knew little of the man or the country, your interest in both will be increased by this biography. The pleasure of a good tale makes understanding easy.

But as well, a monograph as part of a series is the ideal way to enrich a formal course of study. Gradually aspects of Asia are being offered to secondary and tertiary students in Australia in many ways. Our myopic concentration on Europe is diminishing, and not before time Asian studies are reaching the classroom and lecture theatre. Their text books need buttressing. Student interest needs sustaining. These brief biographies, complete with bibliographies, are intended to supplement those undergraduate and secondary school courses and to stimulate such studies.

Possibly as part of that stimulation the individual student will feel encouraged to dispute with the author, delve deeper into the subject, perhaps develop a language skill and visit the land he has studied. By regarding Asia as foreign and unknowable we risk the future of our country. By appreciating its culture and by understanding the contribution of its leaders, we help forge bonds that will enrich us all.

As general editor of the series my aim has been to bring forward young scholars who are helping to give Asian Studies a sound base in Australia. Here is Asia as seen by Australians. As a former Raffles Professor at the University of Singapore and now Headmaster of my old Australian school, I try and bridge the narrow gap between senior student and undergraduate. They share a level of intelligent interest with that of the general reader. This series is commended to them.

K.G. TREGONNING
General Editor

Plaek Kittasangkha was born on the 14 July 1897, the second son of a fairly prosperous orchard owner in central Thailand (which was then known as Siam). He was called Plaek, a Siamese word meaning "odd" or "strange", in accordance with the custom of giving a child a nickname which is neither auspicious nor inauspicious. Often a special characteristic of the newborn prompts the parents to choose a certain nickname, such as "little", "fat", "squeal" or "big vessel". In Plaek's case it was the oddness of the position of his ears which caused him to be called Plaek. These ears apparently did not reach above the level of his eyes, though this by no means marred his appearance. On the contrary, Plaek became quite a handsome boy.

There was nothing in his family background or his early youth that could have led people to predict that this boy, under the name Plaek Phibun Songkhram, would become the leader of the whole nation and that for many years he would hold almost dictatorial powers. In actuality, in infancy he caused his parents some anxiety. He did not thrive after he was born and cried excessively. His parents asked the abbot of the nearby Buddhist monastery to assist by chanting some beneficial stanzas over the little boy. This prolonged sickness in his early childhood may have resulted in Plaek's small adult stature.

It was only many years later that the date of Plaek's birthday, 14 July, became noted as an interesting coincidence. That date is celebrated in France to mark the end of absolute monarchy, and Plaek was to be instrumental in the abolition of the absolute monarchy in his own country.

Like all sons of prosperous parents Plaek went to the local monastery school, Khemabhitaram, which was situated on a bank of the wide Chao Phraya river, just north of Bangkok. He learned with ease and generally gave the impression of being a rather solemn little boy who possessed a measure of gentle dignity. His teachers found him diligent and well-behaved.

During this time, attracted by the beautiful uniform worn by students of the Bangkok Infantry School, whom he often saw passing by, Plaek became eager to join the army. His father accordingly approached Major General Phraya Surasena to ask whether his two older sons could enrol at the Infantry School. The request was granted in May 1909 and Plaek, when he was twelve years old, together with his elder brother Prakit donned the cherished uniform. Plaek was enrolled in the primary school section of the Infantry School and dutifully followed the curriculum through secondary level so that he could enter the Military Academy in 1914, when he was seventeen years old. He chose artillery as his specialty, hoping he would be able to join the First Artillery Corps which formed part of the king's bodyguard and which had even more distinctive uniforms. However, he was not eligible to join that corps and had to join the seventh, which was stationed at Phitsanulok, almost 400 kilometres north of Bangkok.

In May 1917 he received the first star on his epaulet and thus entered the lowest grade of the officer's rank. That same year he married La'iad, a young schoolteacher in a Phitsanulok school who was six years his junior. Not long afterwards Plaek and his artillery colleagues, who had entered the Military Academy the same year, were transferred to Bangsue on the northern edge of Bangkok for the two-year finishing course for artillery officers. The newly-wed couple rented a room not far from Bangsue and there their first son was born. Having successfully completed his course, Plaek was assigned to normal military duties from August 1919 until May 1921 when he entered the Infantry Staff College with the rank of first lieutenant. Up to this time, Plaek's career had unfolded at an ordinary rate. He seemed to have been well liked by his colleagues. He was diligent and performed his duties with punctuality, but until he was accepted in the staff college, he was just a young officer, likeable, but not a ring-leader, well-mannered and handsome, but also because of his small stature, not prominent.

From the moment of entering the staff college, Plaek decided that here was a chance to emerge from his relative obscurity. He devoted himself to his studies and found out that only one other student of his year consistently reached the same high marks that he attained. Over the two years a fierce competition developed between these two, for the one who reached the top of the class would be offered a king's scholarship to go and study abroad. Plaek succeeded in topping his class and thus was allowed to study artillery in a foreign country.

Until the First World War, Prussia had been generally recognized as the world's best centre for military studies; including artillery. However, the Germans had lost the war and it was decided that in the 1920s the French provided the best training. Leaving his wife and family, which had now grown to comprise three children, behind in Thailand, Plaek left for France in May 1924 and there he stayed for more than three years. First he attended the artillery school at Poitiers; later he followed the practical artillery course at Fontainebleau.

By now, Plaek Kittasangkha was no longer using his family name. He had been admitted into the first grade of the administrative hierarchy, which by that time ranged from Khun, Luang, Phra, and Phraya to the highest rank outside royalty, that of Chao Phraya. With admission into the administrative ranking system came the choosing of an appropriate name, and Plaek chose to be known as Luang Plaek Phibun Songkhram, which could be translated as "Luang Plaek of the extensive war". Such names were quite popular amongst the military. In this short biography, we will often refer to Plaek as Luang Phibun, by which name he is often referred to in the literature. (Due to the complications of transliteration of Siamese words, his name is sometimes spelt Phibul, Pibul, Piboon and Phiboon, but we chose to follow a system closely related to that selected by the Royal Institute.)

Luang Phibun, like most of the other Siamese students in France, depended for his stipend upon the Siamese embassy. Naturally, the few score Siamese students came to depend upon each other for much of their social life. There was one amongst them, a brilliant student in law, who became the focus of a critical debating group amongst the Siamese students. His name was

Pridi Phanomyong, also known by his official name of Luang Pradit Manudham. Pridi became secretary, and later president of the Association of Siamese Students in France. Luang Phibun became very friendly with Pridi, and with a select group of Siamese students Pridi would discuss some quite revolutionary ideas regarding the political system that should be set up in Siam. Some of the recurrent themes upon which these friends agreed were that the Siamese system of absolute monarchy was a shameful anachronism and that the practice of reserving most executive positions for members of the royal family was unfair to the gifted and ambitious commoners. In general they all agreed that Siam needed revolutionary changes to bring about a Western-type modernization. They realized that such discussions would be regarded as seditious by the Siamese authorities and swore each other to secrecy. Though the principles of a revolutionary change were discussed amongst these students, they developed no practical plans and their deliberations remained largely theoretical.

Luang Phibun became quite a prominent member of this critical group of students. He was liked for his seriousness and modest manner. He succeeded Pridi as president of the Association of Siamese Students in France.

In 1927, upon his return to Siam, Luang Phibun was appointed a staff officer in the artillery headquarters with the rank of captain. Soon he rented a small two-storey house in central Bangkok where he would live until the events of 1932 caused him to move. Being one of the few officers in the Siamese army who had studied abroad, Captain Phibun soon occupied a rather special position. He found himself the only officer who had the most up-to-date training in artillery, and he was given the task of disseminating that knowledge amongst his fellow officers. In these years he wrote modern textbooks on artillery and regularly contributed articles to a military journal. Also he gave lectures and gradually established himself as an expert regarding field artillery. From all accounts it seems that he led a rather quiet and disciplined life. Luang Phibun seldom went out, and performed his duties punctually. Amongst his friends were many of those whom he had first met in France. With these he would like to speak in the French language and recall their Parisian adventures and debates. Luang Pradit (Pridi) meanwhile had obtained a teaching post in law at Chulalongkorn University and with the freedom of a professor he continued to disseminate his revolutionary ideas. At the same time he kept recruiting idealistic people who would be willing to work towards the downfall of the absolute monarchy and the installation of a government of the people — for the people.

Luang Phibun's role in the coup d'état which took place in June 1932 was quite significant. His main contribution in the years between 1927 and 1932 was that of helping to organize a group of army officers who were sympathetic to the idea of the overthrow of the absolute monarchy. Luang Phibun together with Luang Tasnai, a captain who had also been one of the original plotters in Paris, screened and selected trustworthy colleagues and these two were regarded as the informal leaders of the "junior army faction". By the time of the revolution this faction comprised some two dozen men. It must be understood, however, that these young officers had no practical plan to bring about an overthrow of the government. None of them had a popular following amongst the soldiers; in fact, many of them were staff officers and thus had no fighting soldiers under their command.

It was only in 1931 when a group of senior army officers joined the plotters that an effective plan for a coup d'état could be drawn up. Amongst the leaders of these senior officers were the deputy inspector of the artillery section at Bangkok, Colonel Phahon Pholpayuhasena, and the director of the education section of the Military Cadet Academy, Colonel Song Suradet. Several of these officers had studied abroad and agreed in principle with Pridi's idea that Siam needed a democratic government had to be established after the coup d'état. Their prime revolutionaries, had but a vague idea what system of government had to be established after the coup d'état. Their prime objective in the first half of 1932 was to bring about the fall of the absolute monarchy. Many of the senior officers also shared the feeling that the system whereby princes held the main executive positions in the government was grossly unfair. An

6

additional factor which led some officers to join the group was
the fact that there was strong dissatisfaction with the way the
king and his advisers had handled the economic crisis. The
world-wide recession of the early 1930s had depleted Siamese
resources and the cabinet had agreed to severe pruning of the
budget. Defence spending especially had been reduced
drastically.

Luang Phibun's house, just behind the Ministry of Defence,
was a convenient meeting place and many secret meetings of
small groups of conspirators took place there. The plan that
developed rested almost completely upon the element of
surprise. Colonel Song Suradet, who was in charge of the planning, could only count on the First Guard Artillery Regiment
and many of the cadets of the Military Academy to provide
troops and thus he had to avoid open conflict for the revolutionaries were in no position to intimidate the great number of
regiments which were loyal to the king.

On the early morning of 24 June 1932 the plan was put into
effect. The houses of all key members of the government were
placed under surveillance, and their telephone lines were sur-
reptitiously disconnected. All navy units were given false orders
to be ready to suppress a fictitious uprising in the Chinese section of Bangkok, thus allowing some of the navy officers who
sympathized with the coup d'état to mobilize and arm their
troops and march them to the Throne Hall. The Post and
Telegraph Office was seized. Confusion was deliberately spread
amongst the troops so that officers who might have been ready
to fight for the king and his government hesitated until it was
too late to take action. Most key members of the government
and senior army personnel were arrested at dawn and brought
to the Throne Hall; in all but one case this took place without
bloodshed. At this moment the king was in his seaside resort,
more than 200 kilometres south of Bangkok. A message was
sent to him inviting him to become head of a constitutional
monarchy.

The king assessed the situation, and having realized that
Bangkok was calm and fully in control of the revolutionaries and
that there was no popular outcry against the bold move, he

decided to accept the idea of a constitutional monarchy with himself as monarch. The fact that he was in principle in favour of a constitutional monarchy helped him reach this decision.

Luang Phibun, who had attained the rank of major not long before these events, had not been prominent in the execution of the plan. As a staff officer there had been little he could do. Yet he shared fully the intense joy and relief when the coup proved successful. It was the climax of many years of plotting and planning during which Phibun knew well that a premature exposition would have meant disgrace. The fact that his name featured amongst the signatories of some of the revolutionary manifestos could have led to his trial for treason if the coup had been unsuccessful.

During the months that followed, Luang Phibun must have felt increasingly disappointed with the results of the revolution. When cabinet posts had been divided, constitutional committees set up and the most important army posts had been re-allocated, it became clear that the "junior faction" in the army had been treated with little generosity. Luang Phibun had become lieutenant colonel in April 1933 and was deputy commander of the artillery and thus had risen to a position of some real power. However, Phraya Song Suradet proposed to transfer Luang Phibun to a less significant staff position in the army, and it was only because of his close friendship with many of the leading revolutionaries such as Phraya Phahon, the commander-in-chief of the army, that Luang Phibun retained his post.

As a result of bitter infighting, sometimes open, but mostly behind the scenes, the "junior army clique" under leadership of Phibun used a cabinet crisis as an opportunity to stage a new coup d'état in June 1933. Phibun and his friends had persuaded one highly respected member of the senior army faction, Phraya Phahon, to be their leader and ousted the other senior army officers from their newly gained positions. Phibun led the armoured corps which ousted the government and soon he found himself occupying Phraya Song Suradet's post of deputy commander-in-chief of the Siamese army, and thus had become one of Siam's most powerful men. During this first year after the overthrow of absolute monarchy Phibun had shown himself to be cautious and patient. He had refrained from taking sides in the bitter dispute that evolved between some of the senior army officials and Luang Pradit (Pridi) regarding an economic guideline Pridi had drawn up and which was considered by the colonels to be a plan leading Siam to communism. He had stopped his hot-headed friend Luang Tasnai from launching an armed revolt against the government even though he was sympathetic towards the reasons which led Tasnai to contemplate such a drastic move. Before making his move Phibun waited until a fully-fledged cabinet crisis had developed and until the four most powerful military leaders had resigned from the state council.

The first half of 1933 had thus been full of excitement and success for Phibun, but there were even more critical months to follow. Many members of the royal family had suffered considerable loss of prestige, former senior civil servants had been retired prematurely or had been re-employed in powerless positions, and others had been disappointed when the revolution did not immediately produce the desired results. Plots were hatched to re-establish the ancient system of absolute monarchy and Phibun issued a strong warning that plots against the government would be suppressed ruthlessly.

Notwithstanding this warning, a counter-coup was organized in the provinces where many garrisons were overtly royalist, and in October 1933 a full-scale rebellion broke out under the leadership of Prince Boworadet, who up to 1931 had been minister of war. The garrisons of Nakhon Ratchasima, Ubon Ratchathani, Prachin Buri, Sara Buri, Ayutthaya, Nakhon Sawan and Phetchaburi declared themselves in favour of the rebels. Troops from the northeast of the country marched on Bangkok, seized the airport and entered the northern suburbs of Bangkok. The commander-in-chief of the navy declared himself neutral and withdrew all battleships from the capital. The rebels sent an ultimatum threatening to seize Bangkok by force if the government did not resign.

However, after this flamboyant beginning the forces of Prince Boworadet ran out of steam. To his great disappointment none of the army units in Bangkok revolted and even more disconcerting was the fact that the expected reinforcements from the provinces did not materialize. The rebels let their ultimatum expire without taking action and, as if admitting their weakened position, sent a much milder set of suggestions to the Bangkok government. The government flatly rejected the second ultimatum and, heartened by the fact that Boworadet's forces did not appear to spread any further, began to take measures to deal rapidly and conclusively with the rebellion.

Announcements were made that the recently gained constitution was in danger and the Bangkok regime was the legitimate one to rule the country. The prime minister, Phraya Phahon revealed that the king, who ironically, again was in his seaside resort south of Bangkok, had sent a telegram expressing regret for the actions of the rebels. Martial law was declared. Lieutenant Colonel Luang Phibun assumed the position of field commander and marched to the northern suburbs where the rebels were encamped. On the evening of 13 October 1933, Luang Phibun opened a heavy artillery attack and during the next three days the two opposing sides shelled each other, causing many casualties and great damage. At the end of the third day the rebels had lost many of their heavy guns and were low on ammunition, whilst the government forces, strengthened with fresh reinforcements from the city, recaptured the airport and forced the rebels to retreat. An attempt by the troops from Phetchaburi to come to the aid of the rebels failed and by the end of October, after several skirmishes in the provinces, the government was again firmly in control.

The Boworadet uprising resulted in a much simpler political situation. Before October 1933 many factions including the senior and junior army cliques, the idealistic Pridi and his friends, the king, the senior princes and senior bureaucrats had been manoeuvring for positions. After October 1933 the king, believed by some to be secretly in favour of Prince Boworadet's rebellion, found himself in a much weaker position than before. Soon afterwards he left the country to seek medical treatment, and, resentful at the way Siamese politics had become dominated by a small group of military people, he abdicated in 1935. Prince Ananda Mahidol, a young boy of only ten was then proclaimed king under a council of regency. The princes who had held enormous power before 1932 found the rebellion a very costly adventure. Many royalist supporters were put under arrest, six men were found guilty of treason, and others were sent into exile. The members of the senior army clique, who in the first half of 1933 had been relegated to the background by the second coup d'état, had kept themselves aloof from the battle, obviously hoping that Prime Minister Phahon would be toppled and with him his young military strongman, Phibun. The government's resounding victory dashed their hopes for power and influence.

Luang Phibun had emerged as a real force. In face of grave danger his inspired leadership of the troops had crushed the attempted rebellion. From being just one of the younger instigators of the 1932 revolution who had been known best as an artillery staff officer, he had attained national fame as the subduer of a major armed revolt. By 1934 he had become minister of defence, an exceedingly high position for a man of his age (then thirty-six). As a measure of his power stands the fact that in February 1934, whilst Phibun attended a football match, an attempt was made on his life. He was shot in the neck and the shoulder, but no vital parts were damaged and soon he recovered. The would-be assassin was arrested and found to have been hired by some of Phibun's enemies.

Between 1933 and 1938 Prime Minister Phraya Phahon consistently tried to establish a balance between the civilian faction of the revolutionaries under the leadership of Luang Pradit (Pridi) and the young military clique under the leadership of Luang Phibun. Luang Pradit was embued with ideas and ideals which he had first come across whilst studying at the Sorbonne in Paris. Siam's first constitution carried many of his ideas. He favoured nationalization of the country's major resources and industries and believed that the first priority of the cabinet should be the upgrading and modernization of education.

Luang Phibun upheld quite a different philosophy. As a professional soldier he preferred quick and decisive action to the lengthy deliberations of the civilians. As minister of defence he pointed out that the international situation looked ominous and that Siam had to be prepared for armed conflict. A strong military establishment was necessary to prevent outside forces from oppressing the kingdom. Phibun was not so interested in education to better inform the young; Siam's youth needed training and discipline.

Yet reports of a deep rift between the representatives of two different ideologies in the cabinet are not wholly trustworthy. Luang Pradit and Luang Phibun were genuinely friendly towards each other and they respected each other's qualities. Under the able guidance of the prime minister, they allowed each other to follow their own interests to a great extent. Luang Pradit did not oppose the measures to strengthen Siam's defence and Luang Phibun allowed a great part of the budget to be channelled into a system of general public education. For example, Luang Pradit founded a new university, the University for Moral and Political Sciences (Thammasat University). Almost at the same time Luang Phibun set up a National Youth Movement, built up along military lines. Both these projects flourished. At Thammasat University students from all walks of life were given the opportunity to learn social science, whilst the National Youth Movement grew quickly to a considerable force.

At times the relationship between the cabinet and Parliament became quite strained. For example, in the middle of 1937, one parliamentarian demanded information about the ownership of huge tracts of land which had been sold out of King Ananda's holdings. The embarrassing fact that Phibun himself and many of his friends had bought this land at absurdly low prices came to be common knowledge. The cabinet and the Council of Regents offered their resignation, but after a few days withdrew this offer. Eventually the disputed land had to be returned to the king. A further severe clash between Parliament and cabinet arose over the outrageous statements made by a senior government employee against the Chinese in Siam. It ended with the parliament's demand for complete control over the budget in all its details. The Assembly voted against the government and at the end of 1938 the cabinet called for general elections.

At this moment Prime Minister Phahon decided to step down and the ruling party, the "People's Party" had great difficulty in selecting a successor. Wishing to avoid choosing between Luang

Pradit and Luang Phibun, it made an offer to Phraya Song Suradet, the man who had played such a prominent role in the events of 1932. Song Suradet, realizing that the relationship between Phibun and himself would not allow for co-operation, declined firmly. Phibun himself made no secret of the fact that he considered himself the natural successor to Phahon. It is clear that some parties wanted to prevent this from happening, for in November shots were fired at him and he was wounded in the arm. In December 1938 he, his family and some guests found out that their dinner had been poisoned, but again Phibun quickly recovered from this attempt on his life. Since he had survived two previous attacks, Phibun's third escape gave rise to a rumour that he possessed a certain magical power which made him invulnerable.

When the Council of Regency made their final decision about the succession to Phraya Phahon, they selected Luang Phibun. With this appointment a new phase in Siamese politics began. No longer was the decision-making process marked by a mixture of democratic and autocratic measures. From 1938 until the last phase of the Second World War the democratic processes were suspended. The Phahon cabinets had held a mixture of various factions of the revolutionaries, but already in his first cabinet, Phibun reserved key portfolios for his own followers and both the senior army group and the civilian group lost much of their representation. He himself held besides the prime ministership the portfolios of defence and interior. Later he was to add the ministry of foreign affairs to his personal control. Later again, at various times, Phibun gave up defence, interior and foreign affairs.

Within one month of assuming his prime ministership, Phibun moved to eliminate his major opponents. Many people, including rivals in the army, aristocrats and royalists were arrested on charges of treason, and after a speedy court martial eighteen of them were found guilty and were immediately executed. Phraya Song Suradet was expelled from the country. Phibun also further undermined the prestige of the Siamese royalty. Pictures of ex-king Prajathipok who had abdicated to live in exile in England, were no longer allowed to be displayed. Moreover, the ex-king was accused of having misappropriated vast sums of money and in a subsequent court case all his personal property was confiscated. The judge presiding over the court voiced his objections to the manner in which the case was tried. Not long afterwards he was dismissed from his post.

When Luang Phibun (who by now had risen to the rank of major general) was chosen to be prime minister, it was clear that Siam had decidedly turned towards a system of government that was marked by a strong leadership, backed by fierce nationalism. In the 1930s such developments had taken place in many other countries. Germany had witnessed an economic revival under Hitler and his national-socialism. Mussolini and his fascists had succeeded in bringing about a new atmosphere of pride in the Italian nation. In Turkey, Mustapha Kemal (often known as Attaturk) had inspired a new pride in the Turkish culture. A fiercely nationalistic Japan had proven to the peoples of eastern Asia that Europeans were not necessarily the overlords of the Asians. It was a time during which ideas about strong races marching towards a glorious future under the inspired guidance of a natural leader were an accepted doctrine in many parts of the world.

Luang Phibun wholeheartedly set his country on this road. In the first place he launched a drive to foster an increased national consciousness. A new daily radio programme was begun in 1939, during which two fictitious characters discussed aspects of government policy. Phibun himself took an active role in the direction of this programme. A series of nationalistic plays written by the director of fine arts was backed and produced with government assistance. They depicted scenes of the glorious past and scripts of these plays were circulated to schools in the provinces in order to foster national pride in the pupils' hearts. Patriotism was a recurrent theme in new songs and dance forms. As a symbol of the beginning of a new era, the country's name was changed by decree. The name "Siam" was abandoned for a new one, "Thailand", whereby the word "Thai" was linked not only with the name of the national race, but also with the concept of "freedom". At this time the government also introduced a National Day, June 24, the day of the coup d'état of 1932. As part of the political education of the Thai people, Phibun's government issued a series of proclamations, in which the people were reminded of their national duties. There were proclamations regarding saluting the flag, on the topic of the national anthem, on nation-building and on the proper use of the Thai language.

The campaign to educate the masses regarding "proper" behaviour encompassed a series of measures intended to create a much more "cultured" and "civilized" Thailand, at least in the eyes of those who had been educated in western Europe. The eating of betel nut, a custom widespread in Southeast Asia and some other areas of the world, but virtually unknown in Europe, became prohibited. A traditional way of dress in which a loose cloth was folded around the lower body so as to form loose, baggy "trousers" was deemed not worthy of Thai ladies and gentlemen and abolished. In the past many Thai men freely uncovered their torso but now such an exposure of bare skin was deemed most unworthy. Neat dress became a sign of willingness to conform to the government's campaign for discipline and "culturedness". Civil servants were forced to wear European suits and neckties, women were first encouraged, but later ordered to wear hats when appearing in public.

To those who have grown up in the 1960s and 1970s, when the rules and regulations regarding dress were markedly relaxed, Phibun's preoccupation with suits, neckties and hats is difficult to understand. On first sight it seems inconsistent to abolish traditional ways of dress and at the same time to stress the great historical past. It could be argued that a true nationalist does not imitate the symbols of potential enemies. However, in order to appreciate Phibun's "cultural" measures it must be realized that throughout the first half of this century all leading circles in Europe adhered strictly to these rules of dress and comportment. A clerk, a teacher or a property owner could not appear in public unless he distinguished himself from a farmer or a menial worker. (Even today, when the pure white shirt is seldom worn, people still speak of "white collar workers" as distinguished from those with "blue collars".) Phibun had lived in Paris, one of the recognized centres of fashion and culture, and he could appreciate how a European would be taken aback at the sight of a scribe who did not wear a scarf or necktie, let alone one who did not even wear a shirt.

In Phibun's eyes, there was much to be learnt from the Europeans. They had developed an impressive technology. Compared to the Thais they were far advanced in science, and their systems of government administration appeared much more effective than that of the Thais. Modernization was in Phibun's eyes equal to Europeanization and this was a main reason why he did not hesitate to emulate the Europeans.

Moreover, by adopting the European outer symbols of cultured behaviour and dress the Siamese might more readily impress the foreign visitor with the fact that they were "civilized". Any measure which would give the outside world the impression that Thailand was quite capable of holding its own in international affairs was welcome. In 1939 Thailand was still the only country in Southeast Asia not under the full control of a Western power and ever since the days of King Mongkut in the 1850s Thailand's rulers had taken pains to abolish customs which would lead Westerners to think the Thais were simply "savages". It is in this light that we should see several of the "cultural mandates" of Prime Minister Phibun Songkhram. Similarly, we can understand why Luang Phibun changed the calendar in such a way that New Year would now fall on the first day of January instead of April, and why he introduced a spelling reform.

Luang Phibun was determined to become the embodiment of Thai patriotism, a strong symbol to lead the Thais during the difficult and dangerous years lying ahead. The Office of the Prime Minister and the Department of Public Information were encouraged to instigate a campaign which would make Phibun the true leader of the nation. Photographs of Field Marshal Phibun Songkram were widely distributed, his handsome face set in stern and strong pose, so as to inspire confidence. His eloquent speeches were broadcast over the radio and full use was made of his persuasive and candid manner of addressing a crowd. It has even been reported that at cinema performances his picture would appear on the screen whilst the national anthem was played, thus causing the audience to rise and pay respect.

All these measures may have helped to make Phibun better known in the country but what gained him a truly enthusiastic following was his handling of the dispute with France regarding the border between Thailand and the territories of Laos and Cambodia which were then under French control.

At the end of the nineteenth century, when French expansion in Indochina was at its greatest, Thailand had lost all its influence in Cambodia and Laos. In 1904, and 1907, under great pressure, Thailand had ceded two enclaves west of the Mekong river and even where this river formed the border between Thai and French-occupied territory, the French retained full control of that waterway. Thai authorities had never been happy with this situation and had managed to obtain a few concessions from the French in 1926. In 1939 when the French, undoubtedly prompted by the ominous political scene, approached the Thais with a request to draw up a mutual non-aggression pact, Luang Phibun used this opportunity to suggest a revision of the riverine boundary and the French negotiators agreed to negotiate the matter.

However, before a pact could be drawn up, Germany invaded France and detailed negotiations had to be delegated to officials from French Indochina. Luang Phibun, aware of the fact that the war in Europe had considerably weakened the position of the French in Southeast Asia, saw a chance to ask for much more and began to build up hopes of recovering the regions ceded to France in 1904 and 1907. He launched a campaign to explain Thailand's case, both on a national scale and via a major diplomatic drive abroad. In all government departments and schools maps were distributed which showed clearly what vast territories Thailand had dominated before the colonial powers had begun to take away and alienate portions of its lands. At the same time not only the French in Indochina, but also the Germans, British and Japanese were informed of Phibun's intention to reclaim some of the area lost to the French.

The campaign met with a positive response within Thailand. It was generally felt that Phibun was justified in trying to rectify the border issue. Internationally, the French naturally refused to give up regions under their command. The British were rather pro-Thai, whilst the Germans, themselves deeply committed to recover terrain which had traditional links with the German peoples, showed sympathy. The Japanese were even more sympathetic, noticing an opportunity to forge closer links with Thailand which was of great strategic importance in case of a full-scale war in Asia. In October 1940 Phibun told the Japanese that he was determined to press the issue of border alignment and that the Japanese could cross Thai territory unhindered if they helped him obtain his goal. By this time the Japanese had obtained the right to station troops in French Indochina and they were thus in a position to dictate to the French.

Phibun therefore felt free to act and in December 1940 he sent troops to invade the disputed areas. Less than five months later, Thailand officially took possession of Sayaburi and Champassak provinces, which had formed part of Laos, and also the Cambodian territories of Siemreap and Battambang.

The campaign had been orchestrated with care, press reports had stressed the valour of Thai troops and the prime minister was photographed heroically facing in the direction of the enemy at the battle front. It gave the public a thrill to realize that Thai troops could with impunity shoot and capture European troops. For the first time in living memory such an act was not followed by a major punitive action by the European powers. The great majority of the Thais acclaimed the campaign and spontaneous demonstrations took place, demonstrating support for Phibun's policy of reclaiming former Thai territory. During the first half of 1941 Phibun was thus the generally acclaimed leader of the country. At no other stage of his subsequent career would he be so widely accepted. As if to celebrate the occasion he promoted himself to field marshal, skipping the ranks of lieutant-general and general.

The apparent great attraction of the role of a dictator was that he could implement changes instantaneously, without having to go through a long process of discussion and compromise. The ability to remedy the country's shortcomings by a stroke of the pen must have been very gratifying to a person of Field Marshal Phibun's personality. When it came to his notice that the country's literacy rate was not up to standard for a self-respecting modern nation, Phibun had plans drawn up to improve the country's schooling system. He also issued an order which would have immediate effect — if it were followed to the letter. Thailand's leader simply ordered that all soldiers who could not read and write had to learn these skills within six months. If by the end of that period they could not pass a simple test they were from then on confined to their barracks until they could do better. Naturally, the severity of such an order depended wholly upon the strictness with which it was implemented.

As Thailand's dictator, Phibun drew up a series of measures regarding the Chinese in his country which gave his enemies ample opportunity to vilify him as a racist. Phibun's measures included the compilation of a list of occupations, such as rice farming, hairdressing and taxi-driving which were reserved for Thai citizens alone. The Chinese, who had immigrated in great numbers into Thailand, had been so successful in many enterprises that they threatened to obtain a total stranglehold upon the economy and Phibun felt it necessary to protect the Thais in this manner. At the same time he issued orders to the effect that Chinese schools had to devote a considerable time to teaching the Thai language and culture. The Chinese were officially encouraged to naturalize, to take Thai names and adopt Thai manners, though in practice the administrative process of naturalization was very slow and involved serious investigation of the candidate's suitability to be admitted to the Thai race. Almost inevitably, this situation was conducive to graft and bribery and it certainly led to some hardship amongst members of the Chinese minority group.

We have seen how Phibun had come to an understanding with the Japanese. If they helped him regain formerly lost territory he would not stand in the way of Japanese advances in the region and would permit Japanese troops to cross Thai territory. When the full-scale Japanese invasion of eastern Asia began late in 1941, Thailand was the only country to receive an official warning. The Thai government was asked to give permission within one hour for Japanese troops to use Thai territory, to sign a military pact with Japan and to declare war against Britain and the United States. Field Marshal Phibun rather conveniently happened to be out of Bangkok at the time and a hastily convened cabinet meeting could not come to a decision before the invasion took place. When the prime minister did arrive he immediately ordered a cease-fire, for some troops were resisting the Japanese landing.

As we have noted before, Phibun had foreseen and anticipated a Japanese invasion of Southeast Asia and had decided to be allied to the Japanese. He had come to admire the strength and efficiency of Japan's rulers and the way the Japanese instilled self-discipline and good manners in their youth. He had hoped to develop Thailand also into a nation that could win respect and lead the regions which were under colonial rule towards a new order. During the years preceding the Second World War he had formed friendships with influential Japanese. He had fostered close cultural links by sending missions to Japan and by encouraging promising students to study in Japan rather than in Europe or the United States. It should be noted, however, that his admiration for Japan did not go as far as sending his own children for further education to this country. At the time he agreed to declare war between Thailand and the United States, two of his children were studying in America.

Against the advice of many of his advisers, Phibun rapidly signed a military pact with Japan and thus facilitated Japan's swift expansion into Burma, Malaya and the Indonesian Archipelago. Deeply impressed by Japan's spectacular military success, Phibun expected a new alignment to be drawn up for eastern Asia, whereby Thailand would take full control over all Laos and Cambodia, as well as a region of northern Burma which was inhabited by peoples related to the Thais, and some of the Malay states which had been under Thai suzerainty before the British took possession. Such an enlarged Thailand would be the undisputed leader of Southeast Asia and Phibun set up plans to prepare the Thais for this great task. All Thais were now subject to a new code of behaviour, drawn up along martial lines. It consisted of a series of dogmas which began with: "The Thais love their nation more than their lives" and ended with "The Thais are united and they follow their leader". Their leader, it needs hardly be said, was Field Marshal Phibun Songkhram.

Following his popular success with the occupation of former French territory, Phibun sent troops to occupy part of northern Burma and in 1943 the Japanese acknowledged Thai control of that part of the world. At the same time the Thai border was further expanded by the accession of four Malay states. However, this further enlargement of Thai territory did not cause a repeat of the popular enthusiasm that had greeted the confrontation with the French. The Burmese Shans were not particularly interested in being governed by directives from Bangkok and the Malay States had even less reason to welcome the change.

Meanwhile the country was economically in severe difficulties. The rainy season of 1942 had brought severe flooding and hardship. The Thai economy had traditionally been geared towards international markets which had largely disappeared with the beginning of the Second World War and after a few years the shortage of manufactured goods and spare parts had become quite critical. The Japanese had forced the Thais to provide large loans at terms which were very unfavourable to Thailand and this was one of the factors contributing to a very high rate of inflation.

There had been many educated Thais who had been doubtful about the wisdom of Phibun's unreserved admiration of the Japanese, who resented some of his dictatorial measures and who were aggrieved at the thought that parliament had been reduced to a rather powerless debating forum. In 1942 a "Free Thai Movement" was established in the country by Pridi and others. It co-operated with some of the pro-allies Thai groups abroad, and worked towards an eventual downfall of Japan. Gradually this movement grew to be a fully-fledged resistance organization which sabotaged Japanese plans and which passed on military intelligence to the allied forces. By 1944, when it became quite clear that the war was turning in favour of the allied troops, this anti-Japanese movement became quite bold and daring. Several members of Field Marshal Phibun's pro-Japanese cabinet secretly helped the resistance groups, and the great majority of the National Assembly were either active members or sympathizers.

There is no doubt that Phibun was aware of the fact that the Thais were generally not happy with the Japanese occupation and that there were many civil servants and politicians who were actively engaged in anti-Japanese projects. By 1944 Phibun himself had come to realize that the partnership with Japan was not one of two equal nations and he must have resented the fact that the Japanese occupied the position of overlords. His honeymoon with the Japanese was definitely over and he turned a blind eye to the activities of the underground movement. Yet, he had so closely identified himself with the Japanese cause that their growing unpopularity and worsening prospects also affected Phibun's standing in the country.

How much the tide had turned against Phibun became clear in July 1944 when the Assembly defeated two government bills. This provoked the prime minister into submitting his resignation to the Council of Regents. Field Marshal Phibun probably expected to be called to form a new government. There had been several precedents for this during the prime ministership of his predecessor, Phraya Phahon. After considerable hesitation the regents accepted Phibun's resignation, and by the time the National Assembly was called together to discuss the selection of a new prime minister it had become clear that the anti-Phibun forces had had time to organize themselves. The elderly Phraya Phahon was first asked to return to office but he flatly refused to be drawn back into politics. The choice then fell upon Khuang Aphaiwong, who was expected to be able to handle the Japanese with tact, whilst at the same time being able to prepare for Thailand's new role after the Second World War had ended.

During these events Phibun had been waiting at his military headquarters in Lopburi, 150 kilometres north of Bangkok. For some days there were general fears that Field Marshal Phibun would simply lead the army to Bangkok and overthrow the new government, but Phibun decided to accept the situation. He

allowed himself to be stripped of his post as supreme commander of the armed forces and retired to a rural property not
far from Bangkok. Many observers were puzzled by Phibun's
complacency; it seemed not in character to let himself be ousted
without a fight, especially since he could easily have used his
troops and abrogated the National Assembly. However, in the
days after submitting his resignation, Phibun had time to con-
sider his position. He was well aware that his popularity was on
the wane and that his association with the Japanese was a severe
political handicap. Moreover, the Japanese themselves had
become exasperated with Phibun's attempts to play a more independent role. Basically, it had been only with the blessing of the
Japanese that Phibun had ruled and the Japanese were more
than likely to dispose of him in the near future. Thus he decided
to regard the turn of events as a good opportunity to leave
politics without losing too much face and hoped he could
weather the imminent political changes from the safety of an
innocuous retirement.

The government quickly dismantled many of the regulations
which had given the country the image of a totalitarian state.
There was no longer any mention of replacing the traditional
Thai hand-salutation with a Japanese bow. The traditional spelling was re-introduced. The radio programmes explaining
nationalistic government policies were stopped. Decrees regarding "cultured" modes of dress and behaviour were repealed.
The position of the royal family, which had been relegated to the
background during Phibun's rule, was greatly enhanced, and, in
September 1944, on King Ananda's birthday an amnesty was
declared for political prisoners. The ashes of Phraya Song
Suradet, Phibun's rival who had died in exile, were returned
with state honours.

A year after Phibun's fall from power the Second World War
came to an end and reluctantly Thailand returned to the borders
it had held in 1940. Now began a very difficult and traumatic
period in Phibun's life. Seni Pramot, one of the heroes of the
Free Thai Movement, became Thailand's new prime minister
and he brought Phibun to trial as a war criminal. Phibun was
accused of wilful collaboration with the Japanese and of crimes

against humanity. During the five months of the trial it became clear that Phibun still had many loyal friends, not only amongst the military, but also in the liberal civilian faction. Pridi, his colleague during the 1930s, also pleaded for him. Phibun's defence was centred around the idea that all his actions during the Second World War were prompted by the belief that he acted in Thailand's interest. He had only wanted to ensure Thailand's independence and survival during a time of great political upheaval. Finally the court decided to drop the charges and Phibun was released from prison. It was not, however, a triumphant and jubilant ending of a legal battle. Phibun seemed quite shaken, and the events since his fall from power appeared to have had a sobering effect on him. No longer playing the role of the nation's chauvinistic leader he went back to quiet retirement.

Phibun was released from jail in March 1946 and remarkably enough by the end of 1947 we find him back in the centre of the political scene, when he accepted once again the office of commander-in-chief of the army. This second rise to the foreground was not at Phibun's own instigation. There had been a growing resentment amongst members of the armed forces against the post-war government. The cost of living had increased dramatically and rice was scarce. In June 1946 the nation had been suddenly shocked to hear that King Ananda Mahidol, who had only recently returned from Europe to take up his task as a symbol of a resurgent Thailand, had been found shot dead in bed in the Grand Palace. As if to underline its ineptitude, the government at first undertook only half-hearted measures to determine the causes of this tragic event. Many high-ranking military officers thought the time was ripe for a coup d'état and they drew up a plan during 1947. They asked Phibun to become the leader of the movement to return to a military government, but wisely Phibun refused the honour. At the same time he took no action to prevent their plans for a military take-over for he shared much of their resentment. The coup took place without Phibun's active support and in the resulting dead-lock between the commander of the army and the rebelling officers Phibun's help was again requested. Phibun was sympathetic to the cause of the people who were attempting to overthrow the government. He personally felt that the post-war government had made tremendous mistakes and that it was causing bitter divisions and fruitless debate where a firm hand was needed. Therefore he decided to back the coup d'état and his name still carried such weight that an armed conflict was prevented. Khuang Aphaiwong, who had been prime minister during the last year of the Second World War, was selected to lead the country again but after five months he was forced to resign and in April 1948 Field Marshal Phibun Songkhram found himself prime minister for the second time.

Field Marshal Phibun demonstrated that by now he was an experienced politician in that he did not give the key positions in his cabinet to the army officers who had brought him again to power. Instead he chose as members of his executive mainly experienced civilians and personal friends.

It was a bitter and humiliating experience for the members of the "Free Thai Movement" to see so soon after the war that Thailand's government had reverted to the same deposed ruler who had been in league with the Japanese. Pridi, with the help of many idealistic members of the navy and the air force, attempted to overthrow the government, but the revolt was quickly suppressed and Pridi was forced to flee abroad. Phibun was well aware that this time he did not rule by popular mandate, that many Thais regarded his prime ministership as an embarrassment and that foreign countries, especially Britain and the United States, regarded him with deep distrust.

In order to regain popularity, Phibun carefully refrained from reviving the personality cult and from stressing Thai chauvinism which would have reminded people of his role during the war years. In order to demonstrate a newly acquired deep concern for the welfare of the monarchy, he ordered an exhaustive enquiry into the death of King Ananda Mahidol, whose demise had taken place at a time that Pridi had been prime minister. The court of enquiry unearthed some puzzling facts and concluded that the possibility of a conspiracy could not be excluded. Phibun was thus given an opportunity to further blacken the name of Pridi and ordered a full-scale prosecution of the conspirators. After several years some minor palace officials were executed but by remaining in exile Pridi escaped this ignominious lot. A dispassionate reading of the evidence throws serious doubt on the conspiracy theory and it seems much more likely that King Ananda died by his own hand. In another attempt to strengthen the legitimacy of his regime, Phibun had a new constitution drafted and approved. When the new House of Representatives met for the first time in 1949, Phibun offered his resignation and was duly re-elected.

The international scene had meanwhile become dominated by the United States' global effort to stop the spread of communism. It was the beginning of the "cold war". By unreservedly espousing the cause of the United States Phibun thus found an easy way to find quick and enthusiastic recognition of his regime, at least amongst the nations which chose the same side in the cold war. In 1950 when fighting broke out in Korea, Thailand was one of the first countries to send troops to join the United Nations army. Not long afterwards Thailand and the United States signed agreements regarding technical, economic and military co-operation.

By 1951 Field Marshal Phibun was thus firmly in power, when an ill-planned attempt to overthrow his government suddenly undermined his position. In June 1951 the prime minister was presiding over a ceremony during which an American dredger *The Manhattan* was turned over to the Thais. Suddenly a group of navy officers arrested Phibun and under gunpoint took him on board the flagship *Sri Ayutthaya*, which was anchored nearby. The officers had hoped that with Phibun's absence the government would collapse and a new order could be established. Indeed, the kidnapping threw the government into confusion, until after some days the army and police commanders decided not to give in to this type of blackmail. They warned Phibun to be ready to sacrifice his life for his country and sent bombers to attack the rebels' stronghold. The first bombs missed the *Sri Ayutthaya* but then a major explosion ripped through the ship. The rebels and their hostage had to jump in the water and wade ashore whilst the flagship slowly settled in the river mud. The Manhattan incident, as it came to be known, caused a major confrontation between Field Marshal Phibun and the people who had ordered the bombing of the *Sri Ayutthaya*. After all, the flagship had not been fully armed and a boarding party would have sufficed. The military officers pointed out that too much power had been vested in an ineffectual government which could not make a decision when their leader was absent.

As a result of the Manhattan incident, the military clique who had brought Phibun to power three years earlier and who had been outmanoeuvred by him at the time, now insisted upon full ministerial responsibilities. In late 1951 a new cabinet was formed in which the military clique dominated. The two most conspicuous generals to emerge were Sarit Thanarat and Phao Sriyanon. Phibun's new constitution was suspended and the one of 1932 reinstated so that half of the members of the House of Representatives again would be appointed, and the other half elected. The Thai Parliament was then stacked with military officers who could be relied upon to follow orders. Field Marshal Phibun now found himself in an even weaker position than Phraya Phahon during the 1930s; he was by now almost reduced to a figurehead.

It was mainly due to the fact that Phibun was able to play off Sarit Thanarat against Phao Sriyanon that he still managed to keep his position of prime minister for almost six years. Phibun, now over fifty years of age, found himself surrounded by a group of younger and more vigorous military men who were eager to set their own stamp upon Thai politics. From this period onwards the senior military officers who had obtained political power began to extend their influence over banking and business. Phibun himself had never aspired to acquire more than a moderate degree of wealth, but after 1951 it became the fashion amongst ministers of state to accept positions on the boards of companies and directorships of major industries. In the course of time Phao Sriyanon and Sarit Thanarat managed to obtain four dozen lucrative appointments amongst themselves.

In 1955 Phibun went on a world tour, his first journey abroad since his student days in Paris. He visited western Europe and the United States and was deeply impressed with what he saw. Upon his return to Thailand he resolved to inaugurate a more liberal and popular political climate. Suddenly the Thais were invited to form political parties and they were encouraged to vent their criticism of government policy at public places in the style of London's Hyde Park Corner. Amongst the many changes brought about by Phibun's conversion to democracy was the passage of a series of labour laws and the recognition of the Thai National Trade Union Congress.

For the first time in many years, Phibun found himself again in tune with a broadly based popular movement, for it was on his own initiative that Thailand was humming with activity and that many sections of the population whose opinion had been suppressed were now heard again.

Unwittingly, Phibun had unleashed forces which were too big for him to handle alone, and because he could not count upon the loyalty of the senior members of his cabinet, these would eventually lead to his final demise from politics.

Thus there were the general elections of February 1957. In the new mood of freedom of opinion a rather chaotic situation developed in which more than twenty parties vied for votes. The government, true to its practices in the past, had used its position to manipulate and partly falsify the results. This time, however, such practices were exposed and denounced, leaving large sections of the population dissatisfied with the cynical and high-handed behaviour of the government. Another result of the sudden freedom of expression was the popular denunciation of corrupt practices of senior members of Phibun's government. True to his new-found liberalism Phibun ordered an enquiry into these allegations. It is not clear how Phibun was going to handle the findings of such an enquiry, for apparently Sarit Thanarat, who had recently been promoted to minister of defence, was widely known to have manipulated the state lottery system to his own advantage.

General Sarit, using the general unrest in the country as proof of Phibun's inability to lead the nation any further, began to plan a coup d'état. He knew that he was dealing with a seasoned politician and moved with great circumspection. Sarit publicly praised Phibun and pledged his loyalty. On Phibun's sixtieth birthday, 14 July 1957, Sarit gave him a puppy dog and compared his own position as that of a loyal puppy to his master. Two months later he led the army to take over the government and declared martial law. At one stroke he ousted Phibun and General Phao Sriyanon.

At the last moment Phibun had heard of the impending coup d'état and he decided not to fight. He fled by car and then boat to Cambodia and it may be asked whether he thought of Phraya Song Suradet who had fled along the same route, never to return to his own country. From Cambodia, Phibun travelled to Japan and there he lived for a number of years. Repeatedly he asked the Thai government for permission to return to his native land, but in vain for he was regarded as a threat to Sarit's military regime. Even when Phibun was en route to India where he spent some time in a Buddhist monastery Sarit did not allow him to set foot on Thai soil. On 11 June 1964, a month before his sixty-seventh birthday, Field Marshal Phibun Songkhram died of heart failure in Japan. His ashes were flown to Bangkok where they found an honourable place in the grounds of Mahathat monastery.

Conclusion

Many unkind things have often been said about Field Marshal Phibun Songkhram. Indeed, for some people he represents the worst excesses of Thai modern history. Phibun fostered chauvinism and thus encouraged people to have a false picture of reality; at one stage he pursued a policy of revanchism and embarked upon military adventures in neighbouring countries; he fostered a cult around his personality; he represented Thailand's period of totalitarianism; even after the Second World War he was a military dictator.

All these charges can be substantiated and in this short outline of Phibun's life there is no attempt to suppress the negative aspects of his career. In his rise to power we have seen how ambitious and vain the young Plaek was. At the same time he seemed to possess a good measure of patience and diligence. Luang Plaek Phibun Songkhram did not rush headlong into the revolution, he proceeded with great caution up to the events of 1932. After 1933, when he had emerged as the strongest member of Phahon's cabinet he patiently awaited an opportunity to grasp the reins and for five years he was content to stay in a ministerial position and learn administrative matters, selecting trustworthy friends to help him in future. When finally he rose to be prime minister he had already made clear his admiration for the Japanese militaristic ethos which then prevailed and his adoption of the role as Thailand's popular leader seemed natural and in tune with what was happening in many parts of the world.

It is quite unrealistic, however, to liken Phibun to Hitler. Sometimes Phibun's anti-Chinese laws are mentioned in the same breath as Hitler's campaign against the Jews. The two sets of laws are only superficially similar. Phibun did not foster a campaign of hate against the Chinese, no shops were burnt, no Chinese were in danger of their lives as a result of his measures.

As a dictator, Phibun Songkhram oppressed his enemies, he foiled attempts to oust him from power and he arrested those who were plotting against him. Such behaviour is concomitant with being a dictator. In such circumstances the political stakes invariably have risen to extraordinary heights and the dictator has to be always aware of plots against his life. There is no doubt that Phibun Songkhram treated his opponents harshly, and that on several occasions people who had plotted against him were executed after little more than a token trial. However, unlike many other military dictatorships, there was no ideological purging, Phibun did not condone police brutality or torture.

Soon after the Japanese occupation of Thailand took effect, Phibun began to lose his enthusiasm for the new world order and gradually he began to understand that the close links he had helped forge were turning into fetters. As Phibun was heading towards a more independent line the Japanese became aware of his double-dealing, but before a confrontation arose Phibun found himself ousted by the Thai parliament.

His subsequent return to power demonstrates clearly how well Phibun understood the political game. Before the coup d'état of 1947 he remained uncommitted and aloof. Only when he discovered that his participation would provide the final impetus needed to establish a new government did he act. For three years Phibun was again Thailand's leader and he proved a capable administrator who had the general backing of the bureaucracy. The Manhattan incident was such an ill-planned and unlikely event that it threw Phibun and his cabinet off-balance and brought several contenders for a military dictatorship to the foreground. In 1956 and 1957 Phibun once more took the initiative by trying to establish a popular base from which to govern with full power. However, he had overestimated his popularity and was eventually ousted.

Notwithstanding all his dictatorial ambitions, Phibun Songkhram demonstrated that he possessed admirable personal qualities. When he found himself in jail and there was a chance that he would be shot as a war criminal many friends testified on his behalf and some of these friends would readily admit to disagreeing fundamentally with Phibun's political views. Throughout Phibun's career we can notice as a recurrent theme that he often acted not so much for his personal gain but for what he considered to be Thailand's best interests. This idealism, this undercurrent of sincerity sets Phibun apart from most military dictators. Compared with the regimes of the even more ruthless and self-seeking men who succeeded him, Phibun's rule has a touch of naivety which befits the years of Thailand's adolescence as a nation, when it first began to take part in world affairs.

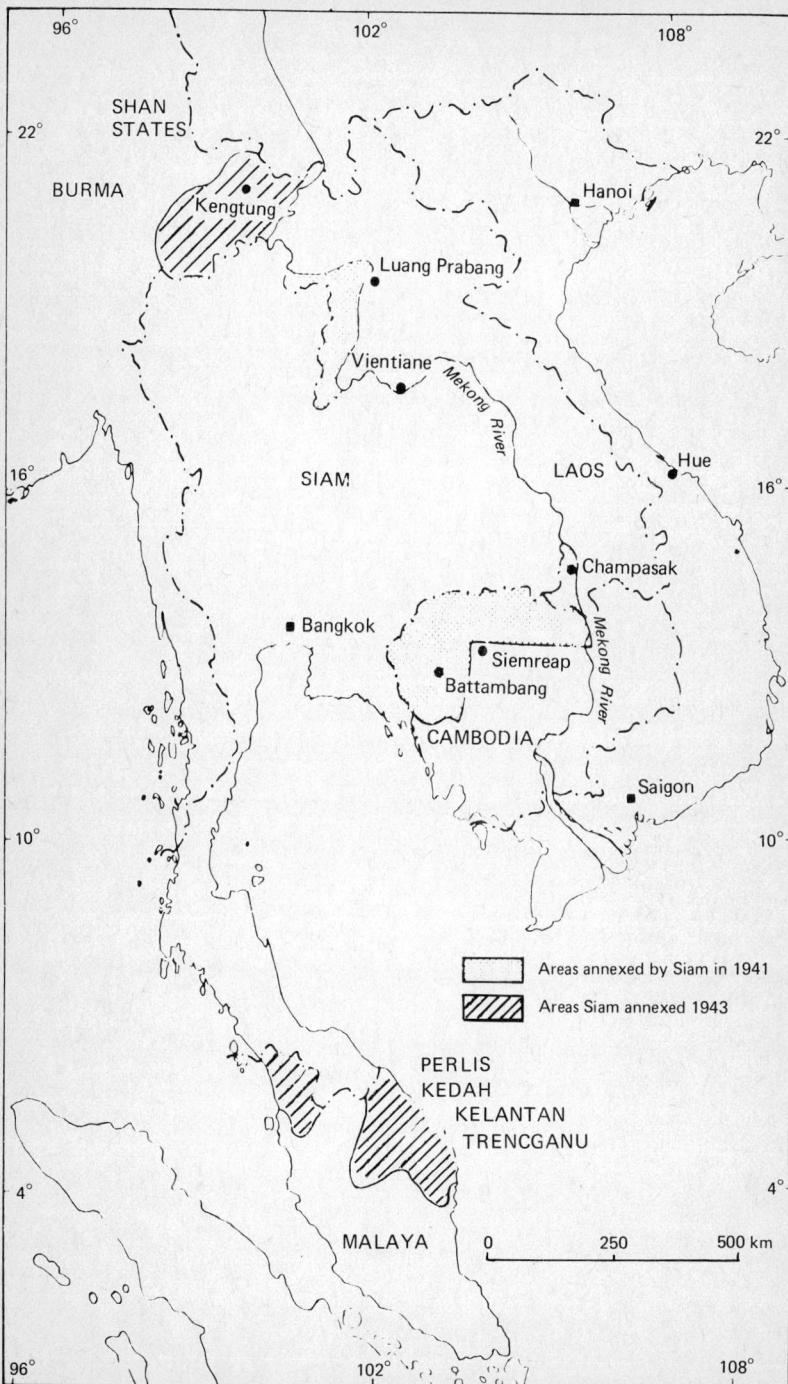

Map labels:

SHAN
STATES

BURMA

Kengtung

Luang Prabang

Vientiane

Mekong River

SIAM

LAOS

Hanoi

Hue

Champasak

Bangkok

Siemreap
Battambang

CAMBODIA

Mekong River

Saigon

Areas annexed by Siam in 1941
Areas Siam annexed 1943

PERLIS
KEDAH
KELANTAN
TRENGGANU

MALAYA

0   250   500 km

Thailand in 1943. Map drawn by B. Batson after that appearing in Kasetsiri "The First Phibun Government".

cal Behaviour (Bangkok: Chalermnit, 1972). This source deals with the various personalities involved in the coup d'etat of 1932 and the rebellion of 1933. It is largely based upon little-known Thai sources and forms the most authoritative text in the English language on the political events of these years.

J.K. Ray, ed., *Portraits of Thai Politics* (New Delhi: Orient Longman, 1972). Read especially the third chapter in which Phibun's widow writes a defence of her husband's politics.

F.W. Riggs, *Thailand: The Modernization of a Bureaucratic Polity* (Honolulu: East-West Center Press, 1966). This book deals largely with the same period covered by D.A. Wilson, but provides many more details.

M. Sivaram, *Mekong Clash and Far East Crisis* (Bangkok: Thai Commercial Press, 1941). This book provides the Thai view of the border clash. The author fervently supports Phibun's action.

Phra Sarasas, *My Country Thailand (Its History, Geography and Civilization)* (Tokyo: Maruzen, 1942). This is a book written during the time that chauvinism was at a peak and it is interesting to observe how this influences the author's outlook on history.

D.A. Wilson, "The Military in Thai Politics" in R.O. Tilman ed., *Man, State and Society in Contemporary Asia* (New York: Praeger, 1969), pp. 326—39. This article provides a short over-view of the various power-struggles between 1932 and 1960.

D. Woodman, "Soldier and Statesman: Pibul and Pridi", *Asian Horizon* 1, pt 2 (1948), pp. 9—21. The changing fortunes of these two politicians are sketched against the background of the 1932 revolution and the Second World War. Dorothy Woodman tends to stress the contrasting philosophies and omits to mention the personal relationship between the two protagonists.

Select Bibliography
(English-language sources only)

B.A. Batson, "The Fall of the Phibun Government, 1944", *Journal of the Siam Society* 62, pt 2 (1974), pp. 89—120. This is the most detailed account in English of the events surrounding Phibun's tendering his resignation and the election of Khuang Aphaiwong as the new Prime Minister.

J. Crosby, *Siam: The Crossroads* (London: Hollis & Carter, 1945). The events leading up to Luang Phibun's rise to power and the subsequent atmosphere of chauvinism are admirably caught in Chapters XV to XVIII.

E.T. Flood, "The 1940 Franco-Thai Border Dispute and Phibun Songkhram's Commitment to Japan", *Journal of Southeast Asian History* X, no. 2 (1969), pp. 304—25. This is a dispassionate account of the steps leading to the armed conflict between Thai and French troops.

Direk Jayanama, *Siam and World War II* translated and ed. by J.G. Keyes (Bangkok: The Social Science Association 1978). A frank account by the man who was responsible for much of the direction of the country's foreign affairs immediately after the war.

Charnvit Kasetsiri, "The First Phibun Government and Its Involvement in World War II", *Journal of the Siam Society* 62, pt 2 (1974), pp. 25—88. An admirable account of the fervent patriotism and Phibun's partnership with the Japanese.

R. Kruger, *The Devil's Discus* (London: Cassell, 1964). A fascinating account of the death of King Ananda Mahidol and the subsequent trials. The book provides insight into how the conspiracy theory came to the foreground. At the same time it argues that the trials did not unearth the true circumstances of the King's death.

J.V. Martin, "Thai-American Relations in World War II", *Journal of Asian Studies* 22, no. 4 (1963), pp. 451—67. This article demonstrates that a large number of senior bureaucrats and military officers disagreed with Phibun's policy of friendship with Japan and how this section of the population was able to maintain communication with the Americans.

Tawatt Mokarapong, *History of the Thai Revolution, A Study of Politi-*